SPEAKING IN TONGUES

· · · · · · · · · · · · · ·

SPEAKING IN
TONGUES

MAURYA SIMON

GIBBS·SMITH
P
PUBLISHER

PEREGRINE SMITH BOOKS
SALT LAKE CITY

ACKNOWLEDGMENTS

I wish to thank Peter Stitt for publishing "Origins" in its entirety in the premier issue of *The Gettysburg Review.*

I would also like to thank Joseph Parisi, editor of *Poetry* magazine, who published sections "N" and "V" of "Spellbound," under the titles "Post Meridian" and "The View from Here."

I owe a great debt, both spiritual and aesthetic, to my husband, Robert Falk, and to my father, Robert Simon, who first taught me how to sing.

First edition
94 93 92 91 90   5 4 3 2 1

Published by Gibbs Smith, Publisher, Peregrine Smith Books, P. O. Box 667, Layton, UT 84041, (801) 544-9800

Design by Randall Smith Associates

Printed and bound in the United States of America

Library of Congress Catalog-in-Publication Data

Simon, Maurya, 1950-
   Speaking in tongues / Maurya Simson
     p.   cm.
   ISBN 0-87905-082-9 : $9.95
   I. Title.
PS3569.I4827S6   1990   90-30785
811'.54-dc20   CIP

FOR
WILLIAM ALEXANDER LONDRES
(1950-1988)

CONTENTS

· · · · · · · · · · · · · · · · · · ·

We shall not cease from exploration
And the end of all our exploring
Will be to arrive where we started
And know the place for the first time.

—T.S. Eliot, from "Little Gidding"

The poet is the priest of the invisible.

—Wallace Stevens

I.

ORIGINS

Men's curiosity searches past and future
And clings to that dimension. But to apprehend
The point of intersection of the timeless
With time, is an occupation for the saint—
No occupation either, but something given
And taken, in a lifetime's death in love,
Ardour and selflessness and self-surrender.
For most of us, there is only the unattended
Moment, the moment in and out of time,
The distraction fit, lost in a shaft of sunlight,
The wild thyme unseen, or the winter lightning
Or the waterfall, or music heard so deeply
That it is not heard at all, but you are the music
While the music lasts. . . .

—T.S. Eliot, from "The Dry Salvages"

I

It has ended as it had begun,
in the twilight of each earmarked page,

where the reader eavesdrops on himself,
the deep hunger of his life laid mercilessly bare,

and all the metaphors for desire nothing
but platitudes and fingerprints, a harvest of sighs.

But it wasn't always so: once, long before
the page peeled itself, keening, from the tree,

there was stone, grey as a brain cell, smooth
as the palm of a hand, and there was an awl

bent and straightened and fired to a point,
palpable and heavy with intention, with portent.

Let us imagine ourselves there, on the periphery
of dawn, a flock of wild ducks rising quietly

in a chevron overhead, the cleared marsh
cobbled with shadows, the sincere lizards poised

for defeat, the pit smoke navigating its flags:
all of nature's operators attentive to the hour.

A pile of gnawed bones, a stern architecture,
the first and last tenement of worms,

occupies a pocket of the imagination, as does
the distant song of the hunters who are calling

for forgiveness from the spirit of the bear.
Tadpoles glisten like obsidian in the shadows,

a ganglion of roots edges out of the water's lips,
a glimpse of catfish whiskers beckons,

but the scribe sits motionless on her rock,
another rock aproned to her lap, an infant

with twitching mouth, sated and sleep-weary,
lies cradled in his hollowed stump.

Like her, we are mute, invisible scribes
to history, invisible to ourselves and each other.

We would want her to tell us everything
about her gods, those dead and living,

those to whom she will offer her child
in the mayhem of the full moon, after

the rains have betrayed them once again,
flooding their stockpile of gooseberries, nuts.

We would want her to write with menstrual blood
the tale of the roasted man, the tale

of lightning, the story of subterranean stars
planted with lice in the burial grounds;

the long epic of the three-eyed cousin,
that traveller with his treasure of cures and curses,

who danced with buckthorns strapped to his soles,
who turned himself into an eagle, who,

with ginger clamped between his black teeth,
foresaw a future of armies, a future beyond

imagination, when the cold descended forever
and their voices became mere scratchings in ice.

But the sprawl of spring is upon the fields.
Deer mice plough through parsnip and eel grass,

a decomposing weasel stares up fixedly
into the burls of besotted clouds as the sun

drags its drizzling gold above the jagged crowns.
She lives only in this moment, while we,

in our armchairs and Saturday shoes,
inhabit present and past, the dialectic

of the dial, the pull of gravity's wheel
turning us this way and that, like dashes

between clauses, like a meniscus upon the horizon.
We are a frontier beyond her memory. So,

she picks up a stone and hits it obliquely
against the awl and bites the first notch

into the smooth, sullen slate of granite.
She knocks and bangs out the first word:

a stick-figure man, his penis shafted downward,
a thick finger pointing to earth.

III

Where does such musing lead the muser?
Pen and paper, purpose and failure,

the dithyrambic songs of an errant dreamer:
all is illusion, all is yearning.

Each moment musters eternity, as if all voices—
here in the telepathy of the lover's grief,

in the unspooled cry of the lying sycophant,
in the polysyllabic oratory of the fool—

are ramblings that culminate in silence.
Must we memorize, then, only songs without lyrics?

Should we grasp only the straws of unknowing?
The world exclaims itself in the sprung rhythms

of the stream, in the brief, aortal currents
of a million pantomimes, in the din of decay;

we are, each of us, one notch carved deeply,
effortlessly into the continuum of time.

Later scribes will say they knew something of us,
of our minuets and misfortunes, our fear.

For some truth always lyres the lips,
some urge to perpetuate even the starkest,

the oldest, most misspent outpouring arises:
being, itself, pools like dew upon the tongue.

And the woman, with her encouraged hand,
calloused and blunt-fingered, graceless,

feels what, in lonely times, we call
the Muse, spiralling out from groin, from heart,

quickening in her veins, unfurling in the lines
of her awkward palm, pulsing, pulsing like fire.

She cocks her head, listening to the rich buzz
of blood in her eardrums, and she laughs.

IV

. . . .

When they return from the far forests,
their spidery beards are long, and their hard feet,

scrupulously clean, bear the ocher circles-
within-circles of success; the charcoal petals,

like paw prints, climb the trellis of their legs.
The bear's eyeless head is massive and fierce,

its odor thick upon the air, its mauve tongue
split by a spearhead, its penis and testicles

garlanded, strung by sinews, around the neck.
They make an altar and they build a bonfire

that reaches skyward, trailing a fountain of stars,
as the sun ossifies the sunk shadows into dust.

Days ago the men ate the heart, lungs, spleen,
the powerful liver, the knowing eyes, the stomach.

Now they all feast on the good flesh,
the grease slicking their forearms white.

She wants to show them her word, the one
she labored over while the infant slept

and the others braided rushes into baskets,
while the half-grown children chanted carefully

to the fireflies to come out of hiding,
or rehearsed the solstice in their fathers' furs.

But she hesitates. History dotes on such
hesitations; it feeds off such hesitations.

Perhaps it was enough merely to commit
herself to that one utterance, just as

we impose ourselves upon the earth, commit
ourselves earnestly, steadfastly, without

obeisance to cause and effect, without dispute
from gods, and with a graceful, numb certainty.

The smoke rises above the skewered limbs,
the carbon arch above them dotted with pinpricks

of light, and the wind slings a cloak of moisture
over their radiant circle, haloing each of them.

• •

The woman slips her hand under her belly-cloth,
where she has worn the heavy slab against her skin

until the heaviness of the word entered her womb,
until that heaviness came to weigh upon her

like a man lying upon her belly, like the world,
itself, entering her, making her solid as stone.

Here, she says at last. *Here is a picture,*
a word for us. Here is the spirit-of-man.

V

· · · · · · · · · · · · · · · · · · · ·

Do we write ourselves into the world
merely to defy our own mortality, or is there

some equation of anguish, an integer of joy,
that charges us to frame ourselves in language

that we might merge ourselves with that simple-
minded psyche some call God?

Impossible, lofty, foolhardy ambitions.
How small each voice's tenor; yet each is greater

than the zero whining at the base of the skull,
greater than the silence of the dead, who,

with their pinched lips and fallen faces,
fume in their prisons, awaiting the Word.

Touch us, we want to say, touch us into meaning.
If only we could leap from our genes, repudiate

each cruel inheritance that leads us astray, that
leads us to collective lessons that only confound.

Let us be Eve, Adam again, or Gilgamesh,
that we might begin anew, rewrite the garden's

perimeters, reclaim our favorite dark.
Though all the old myths entertain us with defeat

or triumph—Moses with his sacred ark of laws;
Hercules hewing out a claim for superhuman will;

Pandora with her paltry greed, her errors;
Cronos, sad cannibal of his own domestic galaxy;

Kali dancing on demons while she juggles
with death, her fangs glistening their seductions;

even Paul Bunyan, Johnny Appleseed, Batman,
and all the rest with their skullduggery or magic—

what do the old myths mean now? What?
The post-literate, twentieth century mind knows

too well how to refine chaos, how to define
loss in terms of decimals, gain in terms of pleasure.

The question of meaning answers itself
with a split tongue, paradoxically:

all is meaningless; all is fraught with meaning.
Like stars we write ourselves into the black pages.

VI

She has awakened abruptly from a dream.
Maybe because it is bright under the scalloped moon,

and the ripples off the lake reflect a parade of stars,
or perhaps because the child has begun to suck

again, and floods his mother's body with sudden
wetness, the warm, sharp urine soaking her hair;

whatever the cause, she pries the pursed lips off
her nipple and lays the child in another's arms.

An owl lifts itself out of the night-gathering marsh,
its great wings beating only inches above her head.

She studies a pile of broken femurs, thonged sticks,
debris strewn about the clearing like a healer's cache.

The dream rears up before her in a piercing light
and with a chemical clarity: she is alone, walking

up a mountain that is violently steep, deeply barren.
When she reaches the summit she sees a dwelling

shaped like the termites' conical tower, only huge,
decorated with cowrie shells, blue jay feathers, bits

of broken bark, swatches of snakeskin, porcupine quills,
burrs, thistles, strings of red berries, and flints.

She wonders why she hasn't a name, something
to hold between her teeth like a seed, a charm.

And where are the others? Where the drum
of the moon with its hollow chord, where

the legions of stirrings under pebbles, or above them
in this strange paralysis of night? Where are the gods?

Trembling, she sings out to the unnatural darkness
as she enters the cleft in the mud tower,

as she passes through the door of one world
into the mysterious marrow of another.

Together we enter with her: it is easy for us
to extinguish our fear, to disallow the dead

• •

within us who spur us toward danger;
for we obey oblivion's drowsy enticements

because we may so effortlessly close the pages
of the past, so nimbly turn to the pinwheels of light

that call us forth, like starving fish,
to the bait of the present tense.

She enters, we enter. Whirlpooling embers burn
before her, red pupils dilating into wounds:

an eagle-headed thing! Four fur-matted breasts
dangle huge snakes clamped to each nipple,

a beating of wings into a fury, its talons
brandishing bundles of spirit blades, its beak

screaming out flames, enormous bull-thighs pumping
the swollen ground, the genitals male, female,

frothing, dripping, spawning an uproar of voices,
the monster lowering its head toward her, its mouth

a firestorm, its nostrils volcanoes, its eyes—
but they are her own eyes, *her* eyes!

VII

．　．　．　．　．　．　．　．　．　．　．　．　．　．　．　．

She has been squeezing the gourd so tightly
that it breaks open, spilling lake water over her.

The dream vanishes into a coyote's cry, evaporates
like a spore of spring snow on her thumb.

Now the moon is achingly near, taut and burnished,
as it grazes the cattails, the calla lilies.

It is her fault, she knows, her failure.
For she has forgotten to place herself, her body,

in her own universe, forgotten to articulate
her breath into the contours of stone, of memory.

Now she attires herself in bracken, picks up the awl,
the belly-board of stone; she will begin again.

She bangs a convenient stone against the rock-page,
nicking out minute chunks of grain: first the long,

vertical line of torso, then the horizontal arms,
the spread legs follow, and between them, the vulva,

her second mouth that calls to the earth like a lover.
She makes the breasts vast, pendulous, like great teardrops

balanced over the rim of the world, over the belly-mound.
And it is finished. She moves her tongue's tip

into the cool grooves and gulleys; she tastes an eloquence
there, a sweetness as powerful as a god's name.

And when she returns to the hypnosis of sleep,
to the unfinished dream with its unfinished voices,

she will feel her bones compose themselves again,
feel her baby's beetle-small breath tattoo her skin;

and never will she imagine that eighty thousand moons
will rise and set before the same images of man and woman

are inscribed upon a slate with such delicacy and hope,
with such mournful love, such urgency and fear.

She will not imagine the bubble-shaped, metal bird
hurtling past the Milky Way with its encapsulated couple,

rocketed into orbit like a holy relic, like a prayer,
plunging into the bottomless darkness with its gift.

VIII

Things end as they begin, in the brief pauses
between beats, in the breath that fuels

all incantations—the flutter-tonguings
that we hear now only in the bloom of our deaths,

or in the glossary of our births, and in the still,
blank places in the mind, between rooms, stanzas,

where time gnaws on its bones and all is pure energy—
things begin as they end: in a freewheeling spiral.

How then to pull free and yet stay harnessed?
We must keep to the page, with its magnetic forces:

it's the deep bed we lay down in to dream
beyond ourselves; it is yet another ocean

out of which we crawl with our knotted tails,
with our slim gills, our flimsy fins.

We must carry our words within the pouch
of each heartbeat, not as loose change but

as diamonds, fiery-faceted, hardened by terror,
dangerous with power, radioactive with magic.

Like the scribe exposing her words to her world,
fearful of every cut in the flesh, every scar,

fearful that the ancient affections of the gods
will be withdrawn; like her we must gather our senses.

We must wear the world like a necklace, a noose,
around our throats, our bent ribcages expanding

with the emptiness of uninhabited hours;
we must fill with insurgency, swell with riddles,

be heroes without legends, ones equipped with spears
etched by tooth-marks, ones whose burdens of stone

lie like pillows under our heads, whose low croons
echo in the eddies of time, in the whorls of air.

Here, in the unanswered clutch of longings that
darken in us even as they illumine our lives,

lie the letters of all our bewildered alphabets.
Evening fades into morning, morning into noon;

• • • • • • • • • • • • • • • • • • • •

a hundred carpenters on the horizon rebuild midnight.
All the lines on the palm of the page converge

to form that one word respoken from mouth to mouth
like a blessing, like a kiss, so deftly it's inscribed

in common flesh—that word issued by God or god, that
breath that speaks us, that we speak: Oh, animus.

II.

SPELLBOUND: AN ALPHABET

For Charles Wright

Could mortal lip divine
The undeveloped Freight
Of a delivered syllable
'Twould crumble with the weight.

—Emily Dickinson

PROEM
· · · · · · · · · · · · · · · · · · ·

All language is a masquerade.
But how we crave its bright feathers.

In every weather we proclaim it:
a loose change in the pockets,

a rouge upon the cheeks,
a lesson the mind learns how to keep.

It's a simple need
a simple drummer repeats

and repeats to the brain,
when all the circuitry's in flames,

when all the cells clasp hands
electrifyingly and sing.

A

This is the silence of the word we've forgotten:
caught in a limbo of throats like a dinghy lost

in the channels of the underworld—soon it will sink,
soon it will surrender, plank by plank, letter by letter,

this word that sailed once with bright sails and
slender oars, that carried the sound of God in its hull

and flew with our breaths behind it into the air.
What word, you say, what word could carry so much weight

that its very absence is a cold flame, brash and dazzling?
Yet no one knows. For in this world, this shroud,

each soul's a caravan of moments that's travelled so far
astray the word's sound that it's upon us again,

though we are numb to it, though we say *yes* to it, *yes*
we say, and the word closes itself around our bodies

in an aura of light, as the sound of the word deafens us.

B

· · · · · · · · · · · · · · · · · · · ·

What sets the argument in motion, what wheel,
  what spoke?
Rapture, or its twin, rage: both are sparks triggering

the diva into song, the bloodhound into howling,
  the swan
into battle, its shock of wings fingering the startled air,

its voice emptying all the mirrors of skyscape,
  filling them
with terror—rapture and rage, twin exultations.

They are the fire above and the fire below,
and between them: bewilderment.

C
· · · · · · · · · · · · · · · · · · · ·

The child knows: step-on-a-crack-break-your-mother's-back.
Hold your breath over the railroad tracks to forestall death.

Pull each petal from the daisy and he-loves-me-not. Living is
a ritual full of magic, fraught with surprises, cataclysmic.

The child knows the silence of the word and the word itself,
though she never learns how to resurrect it from memory.

When I was a child some glimmer spoke to me, some
    phantom,
what I saw through the fog of my dreams, when, damp-
    cheeked

and haloed by my own breath, I used to ride a tiny carousel
of joy; up and down and up it seemed I rode my tinny song,

going round and round myself like the hum of a bell.
Time was a whimsy then, and space a poem my body wrote

in the pages of my days, an anecdote, a lullaby.
But I've forgotten everything; only an ache, an echo remains.

D

. . . .

Divorce, disease, despair, disillusionment: these things
dismantle our days, these destinations, these distractions.

And the devil, with his black teeth and transparent greed,
bullies some into saintliness, others into day-to-day

atonement for a menagerie of sins. Yet, I like him—
I admire the baldness of his slogans, the flim-flam ploys,

his enormous talent, his whinny, his grimaces, his moans.
And really, he's nothing but a carbon copy of the soul's

dark hour, the faces of our fear unvarnished, naked.

E

. . . .

Intricate laughter: in a coterie of buds in April's wardrobe,
in the dancing bodies of heaven-courting stars, even

beneath the dead roots of solemn, wide-flogging trees.
I enter my quiet garden searching for the sound,

for the dim music emerging from under lifting branches,
for its small fragrance tucked near the back fence,

a smell sustained by dogwood trees, trumpet vines, weeds.
I cock my head to hear something: this delicate tinkling,

high pitched, a wrinkling of light foil, a fairy chain
of silver petals which beckons me to the empty lawn.

In my heart there's a hollow, barren place that hears
this fragile torment and longs to claim it, if only

for one moment's moment; for it sings a wild melody
that calls me to the brink of loneliness and death,

and then releases me willingly to life. I flee the garden.
The back door shuts. So Eve exiled herself from it.

F

· · · · · · · · · · · · · · · · · ·

What folly, what folly in the world and in our words.
For some it is a fountain of foolish syllables rising

in resplendent spumes from an oasis in the sullen mind;
for others, it's merely the sigh of recognition exhaled

in the midst of tears; or else, it is the jester's vari-
colored costume exhumed from an ancestor's musty closet.

Who, among us, hasn't stolen into the brackish light
to don the velvet rags, cobwebbed cape, billowing scarves?

Even the bell-tipped shoes, the diamond-spattered vest
suggest the alter-selves we yearn to look upon, as if

being comic could ameliorate the shudders in our breasts.

G

Sometimes in autumn we would walk along the foggy shore,
when the arid sea inhaled, exhaled our ghosts; then

we would see high above us a host of dim angels quietly
descending from the trembling stars to join our stroll.

How tragic and serene they were, waxen and incandescent;
Hold hands, hold hands, they'd whisper as they wavered

like supple flowers against the dark fields of sand.
My sister and I would wander with them toward the harbor,

blinking up into their human faces, wondering aloud
how could the world forget these ghosts, these strangers,

whose beautiful smiles washed our skin in awe?

H

• •

He is so black—(she's musing in silence
   on how the dog recedes into background)—

a mere point in the night, a fixed stillness;
   she thinks nothing has such purity

of will as that engulfing blackness, and so even
   the smallest drop of an inky darkness or discourse

returns her to each word's cramped address upon
   the stark page: small, smouldering brushfires,

or the disengaged boxcars of a broken train
   of thought—migrations, blots, shards of story.

Yes, no doubt the world resides within the word,
   and yet the unsayable is never said

but in the hollows, blanks, gaps, and pauses—
   the way the black dog fades, merging into night,

leaving behind the white light of absence,
   an unshadowed Somewhere, what surely was.

And is. The world resides in (she bites her lip),
   recedes into the unsayable, as she inhabits time.

(The dog has moved back into the spotlight,
   the deck floating like a raft under the full moon. . . .)

Only the imagination is real, full of error, nightmare,
   full of grace, this bridge of beginnings

that she teeters across, while swaying, clinging
   to its fraying ropes, reeling and groping

toward—what?—oh, solid ground!
   (The sound of Vivaldi from another world,

and a green-and-white-striped June bug
   hissing from the screen, the smell of woodsmoke,

stale garlic taste on the dome of her mouth,
   her fingertips cold with night. . . .)

One must cross thresholds, one must
   leap in slow-motion from this darkness

to that darkness, like a thief on the rooftops—
   she is putting her pen down, she is waiting

. . . .

and watching her own motions; she is strange
   to herself tonight, unfamiliar, a kind of failure

in her own devising, an unexplained footnote.
   She has abstracted herself wholly now—

(where is the dog, ever loyal to illusion?)—
   and how the air grazes her sudden skin!

Better to feel the cilia-like arm hairs
   lifting in tentacles, the dog's warm muzzle,

than to know the older terror of lifelessness. . . .
   It is late in the twentieth century. People

are dying from love or hunger or ignorance or fear;
   generations of pale moths batter themselves

against glass and flame: they, too, want to consume
   what they cannot own, to burn themselves up

in ecstasy, in pain, in desire's slavery.
   She looks up at the pinpricks of stars—

those asterisks dotting night's cryptic text—
   she imagines each star as a porthole

behind which stands a single woman or man
   gazing out into the flat canvas of void,

each of their human faces as beautiful and blank,
   as distilled and vague as hers.

I . . . .

I did not want to place myself smack dab in the middle
of this poem; I did not want my face to loom up

like a photograph from its chemical bath before you:
slack-eyed, my irreligious mouth puckered to be kissed,

my jaw ajar, my forehead frowning with ambition.
For I'm tired of the camouflage of words, of every day

pulling my muse-clothes on. Let me be naked for once,
absently present—yes, I shall overshadow this poem

until I grow huge and cumbersome, blocking the sun.
So, here I am in the middle of the page, with my song,

my dimpled knees and sorry hands, with my thirty-six years
spent scrubbing the floors of sorrow's kitchen. And,

what have I to show for such attention? I'm
    empty-handed,
having lived only on air; I'm less than a mirror,

something vague and unsilvered, a mere scent of desire.
Still, there is this common slate on which we merge

like lovers, on which we converge in the moment's eye.
I'm not talking to myself now, but to you: come closer,

touch me, hold me, enter me as you would your own skin
that hangs its brave disguise in the closet of words.

J • • • • • • • • • • • • • • • • • • •

And I saw with my own eyes the dead Lazarus risen up.
It was a grey, cold day when even the boulders slept

the sleep of death, and the land's sharp features bore
the weight of the sky as if it were a heavy glass.

I saw the dead man slowly open his glaucomatous eyes,
the retinue of women swooning still in their shawls;

I saw the swift fever arrive into the veins and nerves,
the flush appearing in a rosy smoke upon his thighs;

I saw his fingertips fill with a translucent fire and
falter as if numb or weighted down with a canny dread;

I saw his lips separate as a cloud of breath issued out
from them like ice and the thick tongue turn in search

of what? What words could he speak then? What
    broken voice
could reawaken from those depths to tumble forth with life?

There was such a silence then that in it you could hear
the sadness of all creatures born to die, and in it see

the bruised heart of each man and woman grow stiff as wood.
And surely the light had been so blinding that I'd failed

to see the man who rose above the rest, the gentle man
with green eyes vast as the ocean's floor, eyes ancient

with emptiness, eyes crowded with shadow, longing, joy.
The way he stood so simply in his robes, so cruelly kind,

made me want to fly at him and tear him into shreds;
he made me want to shriek and cry and wail.

But I did nothing. He moved about the cave like a dream,
and the birds outside began to speak in tongues.

K

. . . .

In Holland in the eighteenth century there was a holy man,
a magician, whose name escapes me now, but he lived

in a modest, canal-clinging house, with his young wife
and three daughters and with a colony of alley cats.

He'd studied metaphysics as a youth, astronomy, and music.
He was a Jew. The Baal Shem Tov figured in his family tree

like the venerable, single trunk of an enormous, weathered
    oak.
Yet, despite his constant reading in the gilded Hebrew texts,

he was not a religious man; he claimed only that God was
    love,
an easy truth and common as the kiss bestowed by city
    harlots.

A good citizen, he paid his taxes, exchanged his views
on politics, and went daily to market for the evening bread.

He gave singing lessons to the wealthy daughters of a duke,
all seven of them each one more tone deaf than the next.

Yet his own daughters were mute, so he taught them how to
    sing
with pen and brush, how to sketch the notes of thunderheads

into rolling symphonies of line, or how to observe one thing
so rapturously that it became not only the soul itself, but

the entire universe smiling from a cat's petulant mouth, or
from a standing jug of milk, from a broken carriage wheel.

One day, when the pale winter sun shimmered like a
    candlflame
over the eloquent houses, and a moist wind brushed the
    leaves

with a quiet glow, the music master woke from his life's
    dream
to find his long-dead brother standing woefully before him.

Ah, but he was transformed bitterly, this brother: his beard
reached down to the floor and was strewn with sod and
    seaweed;

his hands hung like hooks from his arms; his knobby feet
were blackened with dried blood; and his once sweet face

• • • • • • • • • • • • • • • • • • •

was swollen almost beyond recognition, but for the sullen eyes
that still shone with a copper radiance, a patina of love.

Brother, brother, the phantom whispered to the dumbstruck
    man,
you are lost in a wilderness of mirrors, still the raven calls.

*You have adorned your life with beauty, taken the world as a bride,
and now it is too late, too late: you will drown in reverence, too.*

And the sodden visitation vanished, and the awed musician
    sank
like a prisoner to his knees and wept until he was exhausted.

The noises of the day came to him then in a strange harmony,
and he saw, where once the window frame had been, a
    blossom

opening its hundred petals on the wall, each filament sheer
as air, flawless. A bitter fragrance meandered the room as

the flower opened up a scene of wooded hills, meadowed
    valleys,
a countryside of goldenrod and sheep, of slender streams

running their fingers through green ravines, thyme, marigolds.
What garden was this? Was it the paradise he'd denied
    himself

by virtue of impetuousness, vanity, the sins of judgement?
He heard ten thousand voices struggling to be heard, and then

a rough roaring rattled his brain, stumbled out of his throat:
the soles of his feet trembled with the sound, began to bleed;

the cry shattered his heart into a conflagration of sparks—
he began to burn up within the sound, its fury so staggering

and complex, so complete and all-consuming, that all that was
    left
in its aftermath was his clenched fist, lying like a shrunken bud

upon the scorched and wondering planks of his study floor.
Nearby on a credenza the pages of the Kabbala smouldered,
    and

outside the window, the alley cats purred like demons.
Only the indifferent raven, only it, called out to God.

L
• •

And wasn't the holy man right? Isn't the raven's kraaak
yet another version of the song of love? How could love,

with its loosened tongue and its lyric longings, abandon
   him?
Yes, love also lines its cup with spots of rust, a bitter froth.

And we, we drink it up. So, what are a dead man's words
   to us?
Had he been our own brother we would have quickly
   silenced him

without embraces; we would have smothered him in
   blessings;
we would have cherished his pain and worn it like a cloak.

Oh, pity the man who uses love to hide himself from the
   truth.
Pity the woman whose love blinds her from seeing herself.

Pity us all who walk alone enshrouded in our cells.
Join hands, join hands, we whisper, love is what there is.

M

. . . .

I haven't opened up the shutters or the door—
I'm caught in a maelstrom of silences—see how

I'm confined, the ointment's fly, in several stanzas
of this meandering poem; and I can't surrender

to my own hand the sound I search for endlessly
in my garden furrows, in the empty cupboards, or

in the barren arms of imaginary lovers who spell out
their names in code upon my lined palm (they think

I'm deaf and dumb, they think I'm bewitched). . . .
I own nothing but pen and paper, seed and trowel,

and yet my days are plagued by surplus knowledge;
so they begin with ease and end by yielding

to some indescribable sorrow, some thorn in my thumb.
No doubt I come too early and too late to grasp what

eludes me like some chimera of fate. I want to forsake
hope's handbag, wisdom's glove, and, yes, even the sound

which surely must be oblivion wagging its foreign tongue. . . .
But here it is again, that sound, and it is so beautiful,

so exquisitely rendered, so hollow and full and golden,
so perfect a leap in the pulse, an interval of shadow,

that I must possess it or drift into dust,
its ache still moistening my lips.

N
· ·

Noon. I can connect nothing with nothing.
Perhaps even chaos is cause for celebration.

And perhaps the astrologers are right when they chart
one disaster, one propitious night, one happenstance

of glory to the next so they accrue like an alphabet
in the primer of each person's life. I read my horoscope

each day, searching for the solitary clue, the sign
signalling my journey's halt, when I might look up

at last into the stars, connect-the-dots—see, at once,
the bright Virgin standing steadfastly like a silver ship

docked among the midnight swarms, her left hand
    beckoning
to me, as if nothing floats between us but the world.

O
· · · · · · · · · · · · · · · · · · ·

O embodied I am
a transparent lamp

breath for a wick
I burn I burn

inconstantly—I am
a hollow voice

spinning bright and
dark, full house

of shades and
graduated flames

my name is divination
my name mundane

my face a blade
poised between

dawn and dusk
each spark a

fiery wafer
drop of light

that burns and
spells its wound

in embers upon
my glistening tongue

that consumes itself
over and over again.

P
· · · · · · · · · · · · · · · · · · · ·

I have meddled too much with these runes and symbols.
Like a word-queen, I've hoarded my golden tokens,

turned each shapely piece over and over in my blind hand,
tasted each letter's tang upon my wetted tongue,

piously laid out in rows the peaceable vowels,
impetuous consonants: I'm a rare scribbler indeed,

that such sowing should yield this tawdry harvest,
that these weeds should sail up in improbable legions.

I've planted like a pilgrim, with great stubbornness,
with the poet's dull faith that some sacred design

will disentangle itself from the page-laboring vines.
And, true, there are regions of color here:

petals and fragments of petals, a view or glimpse
of possible landscapes outside this window,

and the sound of that voice which surely underlies
everything—call it the voice of insurgency—

but where is the conjunction of word and wisdom,
where the bees lifting pollen from stamen to stamen,

where my hour of small, irrefutable visions?

Q

A particular question poses itself for each of us
during that wan hour, during our time of departure

from the world: we ask, What have I accomplished here?
We may look out the pane from our last bed-ridden gloom

to see the rabbit in the moon hopscotching over
a dry riverbed, and the stars incandescent as June,

and hear the wind playing its sole guitar like Dylan
in his youth—so full of exuberant disdain.

How beautiful the world is, we would think. How sad
to have it stolen from us inch by inch, day by day.

And we might hear, in another room, our friends
and lovers preparing to become good mourners

as they measure out their love and grief in sighs,
as they unlearn all those ingrained, social gestures;

so they begin at last to feel, with every atom of their being,
the hugeness of each death, that terrible hunger here

that eats away everyone's resolve, that grows fat on loss.

R

• • • • • • • • • • • • • • • • • • • •

Language is a long robe
                    woven from the moment
man began his naked walk across
                              tundra,
lava field, across moor and desert,
                         when he looked hard
into the depths of his story
                      and saw the story of the world,
and pulled it over him:
                    its hood of torments,
its flowing sleeves, frayed hem,
                         its radiant threads.
Each letter's shape, then, remembers itself
                                    as something else:
heartbeat of a sparrow, or else,
                         the dizzy zig-zag
pain leaves as a welt in the skin—
                         one letter
is the remnant of December's ice,
                    another,
the knuckle of a saint
                  abstracted into line—
here the chicken's wishbone, the scythe, the rake,
                                          there
the sigh issued by the trout's holy mouth,
                                 even the shapes
stars stake upon the ground,
                      those asterisks
that bring our eyes down to the edge
                         of one thought
before raising them up again
                      to the heavenly text.
        Language is a long robe
                         that wears us,
that we wear like our own flesh.
                         And isn't it

• • • • • • • • • • • • • • • • • •

strange that after
                thirty thousand years
our tongues still thicken
                with hesitation, that
our breath carries the wind
                of nothing
on its moist back, as if
                in the end
silence is the most a word can hope
                to express?
        Tell me,
                how do we spell ourselves
truthfully into our dreams?
                How write
the colors of being without using
                invisible ink,
without unnaming everything?
                Must we trust
despair to teach us idioms
                worth singing?
Still, I see joy sending its plume
                through sap, writing
its tasseled verses into leaf and leaflet—
                joy touching
the miserable dead stump, laying on
                hands,
until the black tree explodes
                into blossom again,
and a paradise of voices ripen
                all at once
into a delirium even the stones hear,
                even the pebbles know.
        Out of the unknown, unsung, unspoken
                world
the known world surfaces—
                out of nothing

• • • • • • • • • • • • • • • • • • • •

something emerges, something still
                            shimmering:
raw, lush, impelled with power,
                    glorious
as the soul of God—
               a wholeness
quickened and embroidered by our longing,
                             our emptiness.
     So, we sentence ourselves to the page:
                          white prison,
cloudbank, the soul's acre
               of dust—
where the power of the seen
                  is the unseen,
its engine fueled by disorder,
                  spewing out
a riot of reason,
          hammer and nails.
     The robe materializes for us
                     out of the void . . .
resplendent thing! —spangled, gilt-edged,
                       luminous
as midnight, ablaze with sequins,
                stitched with
taut whispers,
         weighted with petals of pearl,
of thin rain, girdled
          by fiery ribbons—
ah, the kaleidoscopic patterns,
                    bright echoes, tinsel
of myriad stirrings,
         ah, the voluminous pockets!

S
• • • • • • • • • • • • • • • • • •

This is the silence we're tethered to,
a silence unlike any other,

darker than exile,
overbrimming with hours,

more anguished than Jonah
trapped in his whale,

more piercing than a cry's unsurrender,
lonelier than death's rattle—

oh, this silence is time's best contraption:
its belly gorged with prophets,

its extremities huge ferries pushing
themselves off from shore,

its hands extinguished houses,
its feet wide boulevards—

ecstatic in its combinations,
honeycomb of constellations,

this monstrous, ubiquitous, impossible,
everywhere, cursed and absurd,

most terrible of voices,
this

T
· · · · · · · · · · · · · · · · · ·

And on the day of atonement
God saw that what he'd made

was rich with paradox and
that all the multitude of forms

twisting in the agonies
of birth and dying

were trapped in the vowels
of the sound, and that

he was the sound destined
never to be heard again,

and he was saddened
by his own powerlessness.

And so, with great tenderness
he reached down to each man

and woman to lay a thumb
upon each creased forehead,

and he blew a sigh of purity
into each human mouth

so that the tremor
of the sound

reverberated within them,
and God wept to see

how earnestly his children
on earth strained to hear

what they could never hear,
and to know that even

the green labyrinths of forests,
the great flowerings of clouds,

the deepest gardens of ocean
could not retain the sound,

but only echo and mimic it,
and God saw what he had done

and shook his head and
faded infinitesimally

into each person's heart,
upon each person's tongue.

U

So much wisdom poised on the shelves: books
by prayer-wheel-spinning Buddhists; volumes

in vellum by latter-day prophets; here are
all the honorable sages—Hegel, Freud, Jung—

and the elbow-crowding Poets for whom death
knocked politely on their doors, to whom death

bowed low before cradling in shimmering foil:
their trials and revelations leave faint trails

of dust, fading invisible ink, saltless tears
evaporating upon the desert of my mind. I fear

you and I, reader, are both condemned to live
within each library of years that houses us,

longing to tear free of the bindings and
scheming new chapters charged with uprisings

of the spirit, hoping against despair's margins
that our torment can be revised, our sins

modified, transformed, rewritten as omens.
Yet only another's death delivers us

from the moment of our own vanishing—for look,
here we are among the flesh-bound, the weather

a miraculous kind of lever buoying us up
to float above the cities of decay, above

history's defeated ghosts. Yet when that last,
empty page unpurloins itself, when my last utterance,

and yours, untrembles from our lips
in hoarse syllables and gasps, when all

the wisdom of the world's books has failed
to delay or bedazzle our going off with Mr. Death,

who will remember what we saw, who
transcribe the final postscript of our awe?

V

It is February in the mountains
and the snow falls lazily
for hours upon chinks
of chain-linked
fence, so
each

builds its own small, pubic V
of white powder, a signal
to us who want them:
winter touches
everything,
thus

silence accrues crystal by
crystal in the cities,
too, and it lodges
subtly out of
view in
sand,

where stands of cactus hold
hands stiffly, barbed
statues who await
deliverance, a
sudden glow
of ice.

Here snow falls openly as if
what's secret in a world
is prisoned in what
we see descend,
as if each
web

shelters a seed of history, an
intricate tale respun again
and trapped in a like
transience as ours
which gravity
coaxes

• • • • • • • • • • • • • • • • •

down and that melts away before
we can reclaim it, before
we've gathered in air
or exhaled loss,
or tasted a
drop.

Branches balance the snowy cape
along pinegreen, open arms
as bark bustles in warmth
and a bird goes about
its own business,
breaking

up the silence with forsaken cries,
while the clouds' black orchards
overhead unheave, unloosen the
ice-lacquered petals, frozen
syllables, the tiny veils
of knowing and unknown,
of the endless cold,
of all sorrows, of
everything old &
forgotten and
everything
reborn.

W
• • • • • • • • • • • • • • • • •

Each word's a grace note, a simple stitch
that holds one darkness in, another out;

each word's an amplitude of certainty or doubt;
each word's a dazed soldier on the march,

roaming homeward, numb with grief,
drunk with its dour luck for living;

each word's a sponge plucked from the depths
that we may squeeze it until its meanings

drip their salt upon our breath—
forever may we pry them off the page

so they may woo us with their ardor,
with their fiercely tiny bodies,

bodies tight with heat and longing,
bodies made of spit and phlegm:

the lips of flesh grazed
by the lips of spirit,

a death-defying
kiss.

X

. . . .

Until now I lived, I studied, I loved,
I even believed in history, in cause and effect.

Until now I made of my life a city map,
so I could wander my own streets and alleys

yet always return to the hearth marked by an x.
Until now a swarm of images, black on white,

or white on black, it didn't matter, but that
they rearranged themselves in my mind like words;

until now when the pout of fate in the palm
of my hand leads me to this place; until now

when suddenly my heart's an empty pail and all
the silences fall apart on the page, and everything

is flaming and spitting out spasms of music—
always one thing pressing against another, yes,

always one strangeness and then another, another,
always the half-blind soul and everything

blazing this profusion of stars—
And all the rest, I know, is mystery. . . .

Y

Why do the gravestones wearily climbing
that hill, like the stony backs of our ancestors,

seem to tune themselves only to the wind's caresses?
Why does the conjuring night lay itself down

meekly in dawn's lap and dream of eternity's arms?
Why does the poem circle itself, preying on

its own jagged melody, the broken voice-box,
the snapped and rosin-heavy strings,

as if it would devour and erase itself?
Why, when what we love most forsakes us,

do we return to it, sleepwalkers with open eyes?
Why will history change its course like a river,

flooding the farmlands, drowning the dazed children?
Why do the witnesses of wars, injustices, famine

sit trembling like drops of rain in the trees?
Why does the fury of our fallen years

survive us in the mad buzzing of a wasp?
Why does the lotus laugh out loud just once

before it falls apart like a second-hand coat?
Why does the lover grit his teeth and curl

his toes at the very moment of release?
Why does an immense silence row backwards

through my lines with broken oars, the waters' cloud
of oblivion unruffled and still as the blank page?

Why do the words, themselves, open our mouths?

Z

. . . .

Dusk, and the sun shifts into low gear
                as it lowers itself down into the valleys.

The distance from here to tomorrow
          is only a quick blink of the heart's muscle,

              a shudder of recognition
                   before the eyes close

and night opens its iron gates and nods us in.
          No one chooses his own fate,

              and yet we all do, more or less.
                   We all work on our lives overtime,

        while the soul feigns sleep and the void
              beckons with numb fingertips. Everything

drives itself toward completion and oblivion
              simultaneously,

        as if only through the pursuit of meaninglessness
           do we gain meaning, at last.

The last rays falter on the grass
              to give way to starlight,

and the world extols its lavish shadows before
          extinguishing them.
                Heady clouds break into fragments like
                   conversations

        that return year after year, century after century,
           bloated with sustenance or sorrow,

           ruin or repair—harbingers of joy,
              messengers of woe.

All that we are remains vestigial, half-embodied:
          dusk and dawn, silence and song,

        here and nowhere, there and everywhere,
            the zenith and the zero.

ABOUT THE AUTHOR

Maurya Simon was born in New York in 1950 and was educated at U.C. Berkeley, Pitzer College, and U.C. Irvine. She has been an Indo-American Fellow at Bangalore University and a recipient of an award from the Academy of American Poets. She is presently a member of the faculty of the University of California at Riverside and is the author of two other book-length collections of poetry—*The Enchanted Room* (1986) and *Days of Awe* (1989). She lives with her husband and two daughters on Mt. Baldy, California.

THE PEREGRINE SMITH POETRY SERIES

Dedicated to the memory of John Wells, editor 1989-90

Christopher Merrill, General Editor

BOOKS IN THIS SERIES

Sequences, by Leslie Norris
Stopping By Home, by David Huddle
Daylight Savings, by Steven Bauer
Ripening Light, by Lucile Adler
Chimera, by Carol Frost
Speaking in Tongues, by Maurya Simon